Dr. Barnardo and the Copperfield Ragged Schools

T. S. RIDGE

RAGGED SCHOOL MUSEUM TRUST

First published 1993
Reprinted 2002
Ragged School Museum Trust
46-48 Copperfield Road
Bow
London E3 4RR

Copyright © T. S. Ridge 1993
All rights reserved
ISBN 0 9520630 0 X

The front cover illustration is 'The Elder Lads at Dinner in our Free Schools' from *Night and Day*, April 1879. It shows the first floor class room in the Boys' School at Copperfield Road, now part of the Ragged School Museum. The gentleman supervising the weekly hot dinner is probably Mr. W. K. Butler, the master of the Boys' School.

Designed and typeset by John Finn/Synergy
Printed by Adept Press

Set in Monotype Joanna

CONTENTS

East End missionary 2
Castle and Village 3
Controversy and arbitration 3
Converted warehouses 3
Largest in London 4
No bread in the cupboard 6
Day in the country 7
Evening endeavours 9
Grants and voluntary contributions 10
Limehouse Fields 11
Casual scholars 11
A thoroughly bad influence 12
Additions and alterations 12
1914 Ordnanace Survey map extract 13
Summoned by the bell 14
A job for life 14
Factory girls and housemaids 16
One of the few 17
Canada boys 19
Closure 20
Beneficial agencies 20
East End trades 22
Saved in time 22
Ragged School bell rings again 23

Notes 24
Bibliography 28
Acknowledgements 28
Where to go and what to see 30
Central Tower Hamlets map 34
Index 35

EAST END MISSIONARY

Thomas John Barnardo was the son of a Jewish father and an Irish mother. In 1866, at the age of twenty, he left Dublin to train as a missionary at the Bow headquarters of Dr. Hudson Taylor's China Inland Mission. He was sent to help Annie Macpherson who was rescuing homeless children in Spitalfields and it was this experience which first opened his eyes to the plight of destitute children in London. He was not allowed to go to China but, with the outbreak of cholera in July 1866, he was soon ministering to the sick and dying in Stepney. Three thousand people died in the East End during this epidemic, compared to about a thousand in the rest of London.

By now, Barnardo was the superintendent at a small ragged school in Ernest Street, just off Harford Street, Mile End. Ragged schools were started in London in the late 1830s to teach poor children about the Bible and to read and write. Not all ragged schools had day classes and many of the later ones were really missions for poor men and women, as well as children.(1)

Carte-de-visite photograph of Dr. Barnardo, taken in early 1877 when the Copperfield Road warehouses were being converted to schools. This was also the year that the Salvation Army was named and Queen Victoria was proclaimed Empress of India.

Barnardo decided to start his own ragged school and resigned from the Ernest Street school in 1867. He founded his East End Juvenile Mission on 2nd March 1868 in two small cottages at the end of a blind alley called Hope Place, World's End, Limehouse.(2) The following year, he hired a schoolmaster and mistress to run free day schools in a new mission hall on the site of the old cottages. It was here that he met Jim Jarvis, a homeless boy who wanted to stay the night. Jim took Barnardo to see other 'street arabs' sleeping out at night and as a result he opened his Home for Working and Destitute Lads in Stepney Causeway in December 1870.(3) Barnardo was now so busy in Stepney that he gave up his plan of going to China as a medical missionary and abandoned his studies at the London Hospital, which he had started in November 1867.

CASTLE AND VILLAGE

In 1872, Barnardo bought a gin palace and music hall in Rhodeswell Road called the Edinburgh Castle. He kept the name but converted the gin palace to the Working Men's Club & Coffee Palace and the music hall at the back became the new home for the People's Mission Church which he had started at Hope Place. Both were officially opened by Lord Shaftesbury in February 1873. Dr. Barnardo, as he was now called, preached every Sunday and drew vast crowds to the Castle. The flamboyant and well dressed doctor married Syrie Elmslie in June 1873. His fame as an evangelical preacher helped him raise money for his missionary and relief work in Stepney as well as his homes for destitute and orphaned children. His Boys' Home in Stepney Causeway was growing all the time and in July 1876, Lord Cairns, the Lord Chancellor, opened Dr. Barnardo's Village Home for Girls at Barkingside in Essex.

CONTROVERSY AND ARBITRATION

Dr. Barnardo's phenomenal success angered rival missionaries, Frederick Charrington and George Reynolds. Numerous accusations began to circulate and culminated in an arbitration court in 1877. Barnardo's right to the title of Doctor was challenged, but it was revealed in court that in 1876 he had studied for four months at the Royal College of Surgeons in Edinburgh and had registered as a medical practitioner. So, he was legally entitled to call himself Doctor, although the regulations of the Royal College of Physicians required all doctors to be university graduates. The arbitrators ruled in favour of Dr. Barnardo's charity and in November 1877 it was renamed Dr. Barnardo's Homes and East End Juvenile Mission.

CONVERTED WAREHOUSES

At the same time as the arbitration court was sitting through the summer of 1877, final preparations were being made for the opening of new day schools in Copperfield Road. The free day school started at Hope Place in 1869 and another ragged school in Salmon Lane, which Dr. Barnardo had acquired in 1870, were so overcrowded with children from the poorest families in the district and "badly ventilated, ill-drained and inconveniently situated" (4) that the premises were condemned in 1875. Dr. Barnardo planned to build new schools but in September 1876 he took a 21 year lease on two canal warehouses in Copperfield Road for £200 a year. They were easily converted into separate schools for boys and girls, near the Edinburgh Castle and not too far from Limehouse Fields where most of the children lived. Copperfield Road had only recently been laid out by the owners of the White Estate and named in 1868, probably after Charles Dickens' autobiographical *David Copperfield*, as Dickens was a great friend of Baroness Burdett-Coutts, after whom the nearby Burdett Road was renamed in 1862.

A local builder called George Hewett leased land by the Regent's Canal in 1872 and built the warehouses to a traditional plan of three bays with double doors or loopholes on the upper floors through which goods were hoisted by a wall crane on the top floor. A firm of three Scottish oil and provision merchants bought the warehouses in 1875 but their partnership was dissolved the following year and they leased two warehouses to Dr. Barnardo and sold the freehold to Robert Westall in 1877. The loopholes on both the road and canal sides were replaced with windows but the wall cranes were left. Each floor was made into a big classroom with a fireplace and the basements were made into covered playgrounds. Dr. Barnardo also added a small pediment on to the front parapet to make the buildings look more important.

LARGEST IN LONDON

The Copperfield Road Ragged Schools opened in 1877 with four paid teachers and six paid monitors and an average daily attendance of 106 boys, 100 girls and 70 infants. William Kitley Butler was the master of the Boys' School and his wife, Sarah Ann Butler, was the mistress of the Girls' School, with Miss Ann Newman as the Infants' mistress.(5) The Sunday School was attended by 1,500 children together with about 33 voluntary teachers, mostly local converts from Dr. Barnardo's People's Mission Church. By 1879, there were 370 day children and 2,500 Sunday School children on the books, making Copperfield Road the largest of the 148 ragged schools in London affiliated to Lord Shaftesbury's Ragged School Union.(6) Of these only 33 were still running free day schools because the

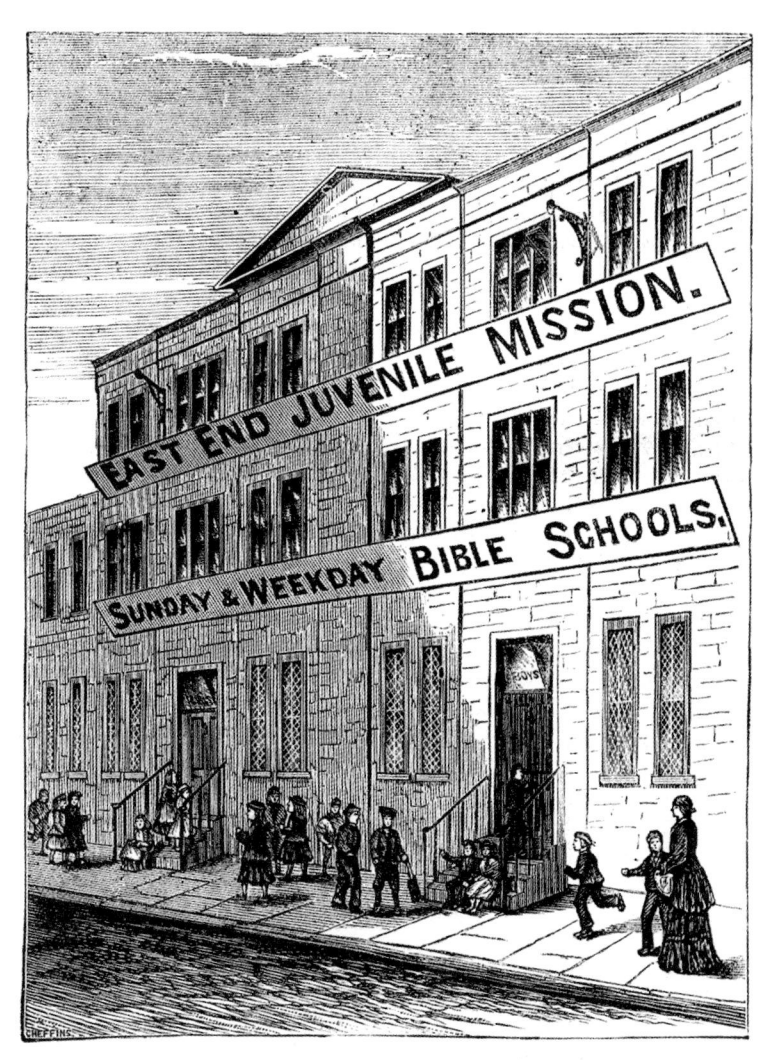

An artist's impression made in 1879 when Copperfield Road became the largest ragged day school in London. The wall cranes are shown but the warehouse on the left of the Girls' School has been drawn without its top floor.

OUR SUNDAY AND FREE DAY SCHOOLS, COPPERFIELD ROAD.

1870 Education Act set up Board Schools where children had to pay about two or three pence a week.(7) Many poor parents struggled to send their children but if the father was a casual dock labourer out of work or had lost his job through sickness or injury, they could apply to the School Board for remission of fees or send their children to one of the free schools such as Copperfield Road. The Admission Register lists many children from local schools whose

5

fathers had died or were "out of work" or "too ill to work".(8) At Copperfield Road, they had the same lessons as in the Board Schools but the children who were too cold or hungry to learn were also given breakfast and dinner in the winter months. Children at the Board Schools had to go home for dinner although voluntary agencies gave free or penny dinners in very poor districts until the 1906 Education Act made it possible for dinners in Elementary Schools to be provided from the rates.

NO BREAD IN THE CUPBOARD

36,158 hot breakfasts were served at Copperfield Road during the winter of 1887-88. The 'Referee' Fund also provided breakfasts for poor school children.

During the winter of 1878-79, the half-starved scholars could look forward to one hot dinner a week, consisting of "Irish Stew, a good nutritious soup, or of a meat cooked in some other way, with a plentiful supply of vegetables".(9) The children paid a halfpenny for a large piece of bread, according to the plan of the Destitute Children's Dinner Society, but in all other respects the dinner was free. As a member of the East End Relief Association, Dr. Barnardo distributed food and clothing in the early days at Hope Place and by 1871 he was serving the occasional hot dinner to his pupils. By 1885, dinners were being served three times a week, together with breakfasts. These were arranged for under the supervision of Mr. and Mrs. Butler - altogether over 26,000 free breakfasts and nearly 21,000 free dinners were supplied. In the winter of 1886 dinners were served four times a week when 30% of the pupils reached school without breakfast and 30% "had only a piece of dry bread before leaving home, while 60% expected no dinner".(10) By 1888, free breakfasts and dinners were available every day during the winter months, when Dr. Barnardo wrote of his pupils:

WAITING TO BE ADMITTED TO THE FREE BREAKFASTS.

6

Children who could afford it paid a halfpenny for a dry bread and hot cocoa breakfast in 1889.

THE FREE BREAKFAST TABLE AT OUR RAGGED DAY SCHOOL.

"They know what it is to have no fire in the grate and no bread in the cupboard; and we find in many cases that food is more essential to the boys and girls than education".(11)

In 1889 the free breakfasts consisted of bread and hot cocoa and the dinners of "lentil or pea soup and bread, varied occasionally by rice and prunes or haricot beans".(12) The meals were provided by Dr. Barnardo's Free Meal Branch and were either free or for the nominal sum of a halfpenny for breakfast and a penny for dinner.(13)

DAY IN THE COUNTRY

Whilst there is no evidence of Dr. Barnardo teaching at Copperfield Road, he did organise and lead the annual Sunday School outing to Epping Forest. Two trains were hired for the two and a half thousand children he took to Theydon Bois in 1881. In his journal *Night and Day*, he described their day out in the country and the tremendous reception which greeted their return to Burdett Road Station:

"We went from Burdett Road Station on the South-

FACTORY GIRLS IN THEIR SEWING CLASSES ON A SPECIAL OCCASION.

In this scene from 1879, some of the Deaconesses are reading to the factory girls as they sit sewing in the crowded ground floor classroom of the Girls' School.

Eastern Line to Theydon Bois, where in a few minutes we were safe in a field adjoining the forest, away from public-houses and everything of that kind. Not an incident occurred to mar the enjoyment of the day, and at half-past seven o'clock, having been well fed, pretty well tired, but thoroughly satisfied and happy, laden with ferns, grasses, wild flowers, branches - I had almost written bushes - the whole party re-formed and marched to the trains, reaching Limehouse again at about nine o'clock p.m., to be greeted by an immense concourse, which at one time must have numbered not fewer than eight or nine thousand people, three of the vast thoroughfares there being densely packed, far as the eye could reach. Every way, from the Burdett Road, over Victory Bridge, down Rhodeswell Road, and back again to St. Thomas's Road, all was a dense sea of spectators, assembled to welcome the children's return, and to behold the fireworks which friendly hands kindled, with a view to bring the day's proceedings to a close with *eclat*.

So far as I was concerned it was with a sigh of gladness and gratitude that the responsibilities of the day were felt to be at an end, and I went home as tired but certainly not less happy than the children in whose company I had spent the day. The excursion cost about 1s. 2d. per head all round. This included the return journey, printing railway tickets, an excellent repast supplied by Mr John Earee, the energetic contractor of Hackney Road, who catered with admirable skill and with great kindness for our large party. I have received several contributions towards the expenses of the day, but there is yet a small amount required, and I shall be glad if some of my readers who have enjoyed their own holiday feel disposed to contribute towards defraying the expenses of our children's outing".(14)

Dr. Barnardo also provided a fortnight's holiday in the country for those needy children in the day schools who didn't even go fruit or hop picking with their parents. The first large group to benefit was in 1889 when 75 children, mostly "weak and ailing" girls stayed with families for five shillings a week. The Children's Country Holiday Fund paid three shillings and the other two shillings came from Dr. Barnardo's Fresh Air Fund, to which the parents were encouraged to pay occasional pennies.(15)

EVENING ENDEAVOURS

Evening classes were held twice a week for the older boys and girls and the Factory Girls' Club & Institute also met on three evenings a week. This was well attended by about 200 girls who had left the day school and were mostly working in the match factories. Ladies from the Deaconess House in Mile End Road held Bible Classes and taught the girls writing, sewing, needlework and how to make their own clothes.(16) In 1884, Mr. J. Bilbie, The Superintendent of the Copperfield Road Sunday Schools established the Working Lads' Institute in the small two-storey building at the end of Copperfield Road. This was open every night to boys over thirteen who attended Dr. Barnardo's three Sunday Schools. There was a small gymnasium and a reading room and educational classes on two evenings a week. On Wednesday evenings, the Institute Drum and Fife Band practised and occasionally marched out through the neighbouring streets.

GRANTS AND VOLUNTARY CONTRIBUTIONS

The Free Ragged Day Schools at Copperfield Road were recognised by the Privy Council on Education and so were subject to annual inspection. One of Her Majesty's Inspectors visited the Schools and examined all the pupils. There were six standards of examination in reading, writing, arithmetic, recitation, grammar and geography, together with needlework for the girls. Grants were made to the Schools according to the number of children in each class who passed their standards in each subject. For example, standard IV in writing was meant for ten to eleven year olds and they had to write a sentence slowly dictated once, by a few words at a time, from a reading book. In 1892, 638 pupils were presented for examination and those that passed earned the Schools a total of £365 9s. 8d. Other government grants based mainly on average attendance were added, bringing the total to £550 5s. 5d. for expenditure in 1893.(17) Voluntary contributions from Dr. Barnardo's Homes brought in a further £618 5s. The largest item of expenditure in 1893 was £846 17s. 2d. on salaries for the headmaster, headmistress and ten teachers. This was followed by £287 4s. 2d. on repairs, furniture, rent, fuel, light, cleaning, rates and taxes etc., leaving only £34 9s. 1d. for books and apparatus.(18) In his annual report for 1893, Dr. Barnardo quoted from that year's official report on the inspection at Copperfield Road:

> "The kind but firm discipline maintained under circumstances of the most trying nature, and inseparable from premises so little suitable, is most creditable to the zealous staff. Reading in the first class of the Infants' School is still a prominent weakness in the work done in the Elementary Subjects. Recitation, Singing, and Drill are very satisfactory, and exercises in Kindergarden are employed with very good results. Order in the lower classes is excellent. The number of desks in need of repair is so great as to impede seriously the efforts of the

staff in the upper division of the school. Here, as in other departments, the accuracy of the Registers should be more frequently tested. In the Evening School the teaching is very judicious and successful."

LIMEHOUSE FIELDS

Writing in his Annual Report for 1895, Dr. Barnardo described the district on the other side of the Regent's Canal where most of the Copperfield Road children lived:

> "The children attending these Schools are mostly drawn from 'Limehouse Fields', a thickly populated region covered with houses containing three or four rooms each, many of them with ceilings so low that an adult of full stature can hardly enter them without stooping. The streets are narrow, with numerous side-courts, alleys and squares. The population is largely a riverside one, but it includes very many hawkers, costermongers, fish-curers, proprietors of exhibitions such as attend 'fairs' in summer, and such like."

CASUAL SCHOLARS

Most children attending Board Schools had to pay between one and six pence a week, and although this payment was abolished by the London School Board in 1890, children from the poorest families in the locality continued to attend Copperfield Road in increasing numbers.(19) This was probably because of the free meals and other benefits and because more poor families came to share the houses in Limehouse Fields in the 1890s, having been evicted from Whitechapel and Shoreditch by new model dwellings and other developments. As the 1890s came to a close, there were over a thousand children on the registers at Copperfield Road but daily attendance was about 600 and sometimes as low as 500. Some of the reasons for the children's irregular attendance were explained by Dr. Barnardo in his Annual Report for 1897:

> "Most of the children in attendance are drawn from 'Limehouse Fields', a very poor and thickly populated district. In these households earnings are precarious,

and there are frequent changes of address, so that the regularity of the children's attendances at school is greatly interfered with. During the summer months there is a large exodus from the neighbourhood for the hop and fruit-picking seasons. Not a few of the children also belong to the families of hawkers, wandering showmen, and of canal boatmen, who are 'here to-day and gone tomorrow'. The percentage of attendances, therefore, falls below fifty! Not merely do children who are so much absent lose the benefits of education, but it is a matter of extreme difficulty to maintain discipline over them when they do return."

A THOROUGHLY BAD INFLUENCE

Dr. Barnardo was providing a school for a class of children who were not wanted in the Board Schools, but this was overlooked by certain critics at the time. Miss Jane Burrell of the Limehouse branch of the Charity Organisation Society complained to Charles Booth in 1897 that whilst the Board Schools insisted on their children being properly washed etc., Dr. Barnardo's school was the only exception, having a thoroughly bad influence and making no effort after regularity or decency.(20) The C.O.S. had been started in 1869 to ensure that only the 'deserving' poor received help and that others went to the workhouse. It was opposed to Dr. Barnardo and other philanthropists for giving too much to the poor.

ADDITIONS AND ALTERATIONS

Overcrowding in the classrooms became so serious that the Inspectors from the Education Department insisted on improvements, and plans involving the adjacent warehouse to the south were approved in February 1895, though it was noted that all the first floor rooms were too low and the accommodation was reduced accordingly. The warehouse was between the Girls' & Infants' School and the Working Lads' Institute and for many years had been used by Henry Crosse, a lime juice merchant. It was leased by Dr. Barnardo for 21 years at an annual rent of £70. In August 1895, an architect, Ebenezer Gregg, drew up the specifica-

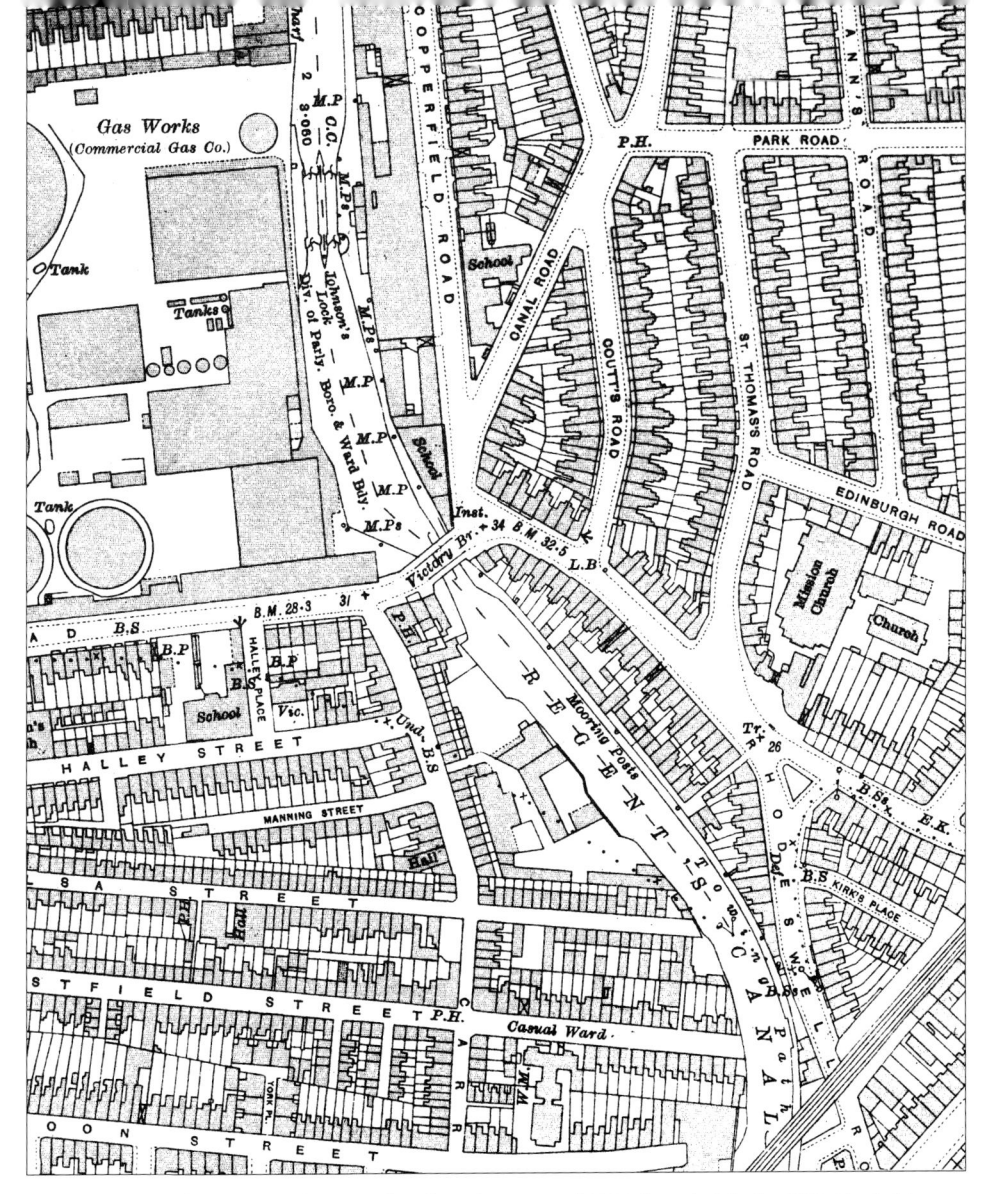

This reduced extract from the 25 inch to one mile Ordance Survey map of 1914 shows the School and Working Lads' Institute at the end of Copperfield Road. Most of the ragged school children walked over the Victory Bridge from the smallest houses in Limehouse Fields. Carr Street runs across all the streets in this district and was known locally as "Donkey Row" because there were so many costers who kept donkeys in their backyards. The Hall in Carr Street was Dorcas House where Dr. Barnardo's Deaconesses ran Mothers' Meetings from 1887 to 1897. Just the other side of Carr Street is a large triangular space next to the Regent's Canal where the Woodchopping Brigade had been based. Not far away on the other side of the Canal is Dr. Barnardo's People's Mission Church behind the famous Edinburgh Castle on Rhodeswell Road. The adjacent Church was St. Ann's Iron Hall where the girls and infants went to school during the building work in 1895-96. The area of this map extract is shown on the modern map of Central Tower Hamlets on page 34.

tions for the additions and alterations. These included new fireplaces in the old lime juice warehouse and new doorways in the dividing wall to make it an extension of the Girls' & Infants' School. The walls of this and the Boys' School were to be raised by four feet to give more height to the top floor classrooms. The roof and pediment had to be re-built and granolithic floors laid in the basement playgrounds. Two new granolithic staircases on Dorman Long steel girders were to be fixed on either side of the dividing wall between the two Schools, and new doorways cut in the wall at each landing. New fireplaces and larger windows were to be fitted in places and 2,000 School Board regulation hat & coat pegs fixed up. The Working Lads' Institute was to be repaired and all walls distempered pale primrose stone colour with chocolate dado throughout. (21)

SUMMONED BY THE BELL

During the building work, the girls and infants were transferred to St. Ann's Iron Hall and the boys were taught in the Burdett Dormitory.(22) The children returned to their Schools on 8th June 1896, doubtless summoned by the new bell on the pediment. Dr. Barnardo's Annual Report for this year gives the following information:

Day School Children under instruction	1,075
Older Boys and Girls attending evening classes	178
Children in attendance at Sunday School	2,460
Children sent out into the country for a fortnight's holiday	157
Cases inquired into for Relief and Soup Dinners supplied	1,560
Children's Free Meals supplied	65,542
Boots and old garments supplied to necessitous cases	8,040
Boys and Girls assisted with suitable outfits upon entering their first situation	27
Teachers	13

A JOB FOR LIFE

Pupils leaving the Schools were not only provided with suitable clothing for their first job, they were encouraged to keep it: for instance, in 1897 prizes were given to 46 former Night School

Boys from the Ragged School chopping firewood in the yard at the Youths' Labour House in about 1893. The older boy tying up the bundles on the right is a uniformed resident. His sailor's cap bore the initials Y.L.H.

scholars for retaining their situations, 28 of whom had done so for three and five years. Many of the boys were found work in either Dr. Barnardo's Woodchopping Brigade or his City Messenger Brigade. Like others in the Ragged School Movement, Dr. Barnardo was very conscious of the need to provide employment for his old pupils, especially the boys who often found it difficult to get a job. He started his Woodchopping Brigade in 1868 for his older boys at Hope Place. They chopped wood and made bundles of firewood for sale. This was ideal for boys who went fruit and hop picking in the summer and needed a temporary job to help their families through the winter months. From 1873 the Brigade was situated on the Regent's Canal at Rhodeswell Wharf, Carr Street, where Baltic timber was unloaded and chopped into firewood. In 1883, the work was transferred to the Youths' Labour House,

E. E. J. M.—Home for Working & Destitue Lads.

No. 11.—A Group of City Messengers with their Young Inspector

One of an early set of picture cards sold in aid of the Mission. It shows a group of former Ragged School boys in the backyard of the City Messenger Brigade headquarters at 18 Stepney Causeway.

Commercial Road, where it was undertaken by the seventeen year old inmates though 'out-of-door boys' from the Ragged School were also employed there.(23) The most successful of Dr. Barnardo's employment agencies for his old Ragged School boys was the City Messenger Brigade, founded in 1870 for:

"lads of good character living at home with one or both parents." (24)

The uniformed boys, who had to be of respectable appearance and able to read sufficiently well, delivered messages, letters and parcels for merchants and tradesmen in the City. They earned several shillings a week, from which the cost of their uniform was deducted in small amounts . After their eighteen months in the Brigade most of them managed to get a regular job in the City.

FACTORY GIRLS AND HOUSEMAIDS

The girls had far less difficulty finding work as there was a great demand for cheap girl labour at Bryant & May's and the other match factories and at hundreds of other factories making chocolates, sweets, jams and pickles and various other articles. Their wages supported many a family during periods of high male unemployment in the docks and other places like gasworks, where casual work was on a seasonal basis. Whilst recognising this fact in his Annual Report for 1882-1883, Dr. Barnardo was concerned about the girls' behaviour:

> "As may be imagined, factory life among young girls, though it appears to be a social necessity, is not conducive to the cultivation of gentle manners, nor a quiet and tractable spirit..."

It was to foster these and other domestic virtues among his old girls that Dr. Barnardo had established the Factory Girls' Club & Institute in 1877. Although the Club was very successful, it was thought that proper household training for domestic service would ensure that when the girls got married they would make better housewives than their mothers. So, in 1883, Dr. Barnardo established his Servants' Free Registry and Training Home in Bow Road. The Deaconesses encouraged the fifteen year olds at the Club to give up factory work and sign on at the Training Home. Here they lived and trained for two or three months under the able superintendence of Miss Kennedy. They spent a lot of their time washing, mending and ironing boys' clothes from the Home in Stepney Causeway. They then went out as day servants to one of the big houses in the East End and were eventually found a permanent situation.

ONE OF THE FEW

Superintendents of ragged schools were encouraged to contribute a short report to the monthly magazine In His Name: The Record of the R.S.U. and Shaftesbury Society. In December 1903, the following report appeared from Copperfield Road when it was one of the five remaining ragged day schools in London:

> "COPPERFIELD ROAD.- The above school has been carried on for more than thirty-six years, and shows for each year a direct advance. The work began in a small four-roomed cottage in Pedlar's Orchard (now extinct), then removed to Hope Place, and later on to the present building in Copperfield Road. The work is little known outside the locality of Donkey Row and

Limehouse Fields, but has been a great boon to the neighbourhood during its existence. The agencies, which are many, are all in a healthy condition and full activity. The day school, one of the few remaining efforts of old-time Ragged School work, is in a prosperous state, there being at the present time 900 children on the books, with an average of nearly 700, requiring seventeen teachers. Then in the Sunday School and services are gathered in on the Lord's Day 2,000 scholars, with sixty-five teachers, two-thirds of whom are old scholars. It is gratifying to know that many former scholars are now out in the Master's service at home and abroad, occupying positions of clergymen, pastors, evangelists, and superintendents of Missions, thus spreading, indirectly, the work far and wide. In union with the School there are the usual agencies - Night Classes, Factory Girls' Club, and Sewing Classes, Bands of Hope, gymnasium etc. The special effort for this session is a monthly service, held on the first Wednesday only. Boys and girls over nine years are admitted, when addresses, vocal and instrumental music, lantern lectures etc., have been given. At the first meeting hundreds had to be turned away. These special gatherings are held at the Edinboro' Castle, Limehouse."

1903 also saw the passage of the London Education Bill which transferred responsibility for the whole of London's public education to the London County Council. In 1904, the L.C.C. took over the maintenance of 521 Board Schools and 438 voluntary schools, subject to a satisfactory inspection and survey of the buildings. Copperfield Road was one of ninety-two schools found to be unsuitable for the purposes of elementary education. In particular, the following defects were noted:

"The rooms are all low, irregular in shape and cut up by columns...urinals in a dilapidated condition...playgrounds are inadequate and there is no accommodation for the teachers in the infants' department"

On 30th May 1905, the Council resolved that they would cease to maintain Barnardo's Free School after the children had been provided with other accommodation.

CANADA BOYS

The Council had in fact already stopped paying the masters' salaries because of a drastic change in the admissions policy at Copperfield Road. 251 local boys had been turned out in October 1904 to make way for boys from Leopold House.(25) This was a Dr. Barnardo Home in Burdett Road for ten to thirteen year olds who were educated on the premises and finally shipped off to Canada each summer. The Local Government Board thought that the boys "should have more outdoor exercise and not be confined entirely to the premises in which they reside". As a result, their school was closed and they were sent to Copperfield Road. Although the L.C.C. were not informed, they knew of the change but did nothing until January 1905, when they stopped the masters' salaries as the L.C.C. were no longer responsible for supporting what had become an Institutional School. In June 1905, the Copperfield Road Managers appealed to the Board of Education, stating that they had been compelled to pay the masters' salaries, and enclosing correspondence which claimed that the Headmaster was under their instructions to take local boys, 34 of whom had been admitted since February. Officials at the Board of Education were of the opinion that Copperfield Road was clearly not an Institutional School within the meaning of the 1902 Act and wrote to the L.C.C. demanding that they maintain the school "and if not to request why it should receive exceptional treatment". The L.C.C. agreed to do so from 4th July, "without expressing an opinion as to the unusual action of the managers in excluding a large number of children and of subsequently admitting a small number". It was noted in Whitehall that neither the Managers nor the L.C.C. figured very well in the affair and that the Council wished to punish the former for not having consulted them in the first instance. The Board hoped the Council would maintain the School from 1st January to 4th July 1905, which they finally consented to in October 1905.(26)

Dr. Barnardo had died just a few weeks before this decision and his body lay in state for four days at the Edinburgh Castle. On the day of the funeral, houses were draped in black and flags flown at half-mast as a vast procession followed his coffin through the crowded streets of the East End to Liverpool Street. From the station it was taken by special train to the Girls' Village Home, where his cremated remains were later buried.

Most of the local boys given notice in 1904 probably found places at Council Schools in the vicinity, but doubtless missed their free meals. Leopold House boys continued to attend the School until it was closed by the L.C.C. in 1908. So as well as teaching local children during its last four years, Copperfield Road also taught the younger Barnardo boys who were sent to Canada.(27)

CLOSURE

In January 1907, the L.C.C. proposed a massive reduction in the number of pupils, mainly because the first floor classrooms were too low. By the end of the year, the Board of Education had agreed to their unsuitability and arrangements were made for the Leopold House boys to go to Single Street and South Grove Council Schools. The boys moved out sometime after March 1908 and the first floor classrooms were abandoned. To accommodate some of the remaining girls and infants, the L.C.C. was busily erecting a new school in temporary iron buildings in Ocean Street. Once these were up the Copperfield Road School was closed on 5th June 1908 and 141 girls and infants went to the 'iron school'. Another large group of 136 went to the adjacent Trafalgar Square School, near White Horse Lane. 73 children went to other schools and 63 either left school, moved from the neighbourhood or were unable to attend school.(28) Of the ragged day schools in London, Copperfield Road was the last but one to close. It was followed by George Yard, Whitechapel in 1910.

BENEFICIAL AGENCIES

The Copperfield Road premises were renamed Edinburgh Castle Mission School and used for Sunday Schools and services, evening classes under the inspection of the Science and Art Department, classes for factory girls on Tuesdays and Thursdays and various clubs and bands. The Annual Report for 1909 records that:

> "a generous friend gave a Christmas Treat to 2,500 children at the Sunday School, under the auspices of the Duke and Duchess of Somerset, Mrs. Barnardo and others".

Boys and girls outside the Sunday School in December 1909, waving their invitation cards to the Christmas Treat at the Edinburgh Castle. The day schools had just closed the year before and the Boys' and Girls' entrances are clearly seen with the 1895 extension on the left. This former warehouse is now the Ragged School Museum at 48 Copperfield Road.

This took place on the Twelfth Day of Christmas, 5th January 1910 at the Edinburgh Castle. An article in *Night and Day* for March 1910 recorded that:

> "There was an ample meal, a distribution of prizes afterwards to the guests and a perfectly delightful Christmas tree, the gift of Mr. H. Gordon Selfridge".

The 1909 and later Reports refer to the Copperfield Road Mission School where the "numerous agencies for the benefit of children in the neighbourhood" continued until early 1915, when they moved to the Edinburgh Castle. Here the Sunday School and its various agencies were "under the superintendency of Messrs. W. K. Butler and J. H. Winn" with a teaching staff of thirty.(29) The Factory Girls' Club was the last to leave for the Castle "on expiration of lease" in 1916.

EAST END TRADES

For the next thirty years, the old ragged school buildings were taken over by the 'rag trade' and occupied mostly by Jewish clothing manufacturers. The most important was the firm of Harris & Woolf which made men's suits at 46 Copperfield Road from 1925 to 1937. This street number dates from 1903 when the original ragged school buildings were re-numbered 46, the 1895 extension re-numbered 48 and the old Working Lads' Institute re-numbered 50 Copperfield Road. After 1937, various floors at 46 Copperfield Road were let to different clothing firms, including a number of important women's coat manufacturers.

From about 1945 to 1951, 46 Copperfield Road was occupied by rag merchants W. R. Dick & Sons Ltd. who received rags from all over London for sorting and selling to paper mills and textile firms in the north of England. Dick's were followed by another firm of rag merchants until 1953 when a fire broke out and destroyed the original wooden roof trusses. Although new lightweight roofs on steel trusses were built, they remain hidden behind the parapet. The front of the building is the same today as when it was the ragged school. The long sign boards have gone, leaving lighter brickwork under the upper windows of 46 Copperfield Road, but the school bell is still on the pediment and the warehouse wall cranes, as left by Dr. Barnardo in 1877, are still in position. From about 1958 to 1963, the old ragged school was occupied by the furniture-making firm of J. Ellman & Son Ltd. Between 1967 and 1984, it was a linen dealers and afterwards a government surplus warehouse.

SAVED IN TIME

Copperfield Road was to have been demolished for an extension to Mile End Park but a case for the retention of 46, 48 and 50 Copperfield Road was made on the grounds that they were the only Dr. Barnardo buildings still in the heart of the area where he began his pioneering work for all destitute children and founded the largest of the nineteenth century philanthropic organisations. As such, it was believed that 46 and 48 Copperfield Road, that once housed the largest ragged school in London, would make an ideal home for a museum about the East End and the history of education and youth provision in London. Also, that the old Working Lads' Institute at 50 Copperfield Road would convert to a community resource centre. To this end, the Ragged School Museum Trust was set up in 1983, secured the listing of 46 and 48 Copperfield Road as Grade II historic buildings in 1985 and by early 1986 had acquired the freeholds of all three properties with a grant from the Greater London Council Arts & Recreation Committee.

RAGGED SCHOOL BELL RINGS AGAIN

In 1988 work started on the repair and conversion of 48 Copperfield Road funded by the Department of the Environment and London City Action Team, London Borough of Tower Hamlets and English Heritage, with a loan from the Architectural Heritage Fund.(30) This building was the old lime juice warehouse and became part of the Girls' and Infants' School when new doorways were cut in the dividing wall. After closure the doorways were bricked up but those on the first and second floors have been re-opened as new doorways for the museum. A Victorian classroom has been created on the first floor, a shop and curator's office on the ground floor and a cafe in the basement with a re-opened doorway on to the canal towpath. A new cornice was placed on the plain brick parapet which had been re-built after suffering bomb blast damage in the Blitz. The museum at 48 Copperfield Road has been painted throughout in the old ragged school colours of chocolate brown and primrose yellow. On 7th April 1990 it was officially opened by Lady Wagner ringing the old school bell for the first time since 1916. School parties from all over London now experience Victorian lessons in our recreated classroom.

In July 1992, the Civic Trust presented the Ragged School Museum Trust with a Special Mention Award for making a building conversion of benefit to the community.

NOTES

(1) In London, there were a few Sunday schools for poor children before 1835 but it was the London City Missionaries who started the first sunday schools specifically for 'ragged' children. By the early 1840s they had acquired the name 'ragged schools'. At the request of his friend, Angela Burdett Coutts, Charles Dickens visited the Field Lane Ragged School in 1843. The outcast children inspired him to write *A Christmas Carol*, the first of several Christmas stories. Nineteen of these schools formed a London organisation called the Ragged School Union in 1844, under the Presidency of Lord Shaftesbury from 1845 to 1885. By 1846, there were about forty ragged Sunday schools and four ragged day schools providing free education. At its height in 1869 the R.S.U. included 272 ragged Sunday schools and 195 ragged day schools.

(2) This was one of the first organisations to include 'East End' in its title. The term 'East-end' was first used in print by Henry Mayhew in 1849 for the area to the east of the City of London which was then built up as far as Blackwall, near the mouth of the River Lea.

(3) Dr. Barnardo claimed in his Annual Report for 1874-75 that his was the first institution to go out at night searching for destitute boys and girls. It was also the first to help all destitute children regardless of race, creed, sex or physical condition.

(4) *Annual Report* for 1874-75.

(5) The Butlers were in charge for at least fourteen years up to about 1891. During the early 1880s they lived at 16 Addington Road, Bow. Miss Newman was Infants' mistress for about four years. In 1883 the Infants' mistress was Miss Elizabeth Brown (Trades' and Court Directories).

(6) It is appropriate that the largest ragged school in London was situated in and named after a road which was probably named after Charles Dickens' autobiographical novel, as Dickens was one of the earliest and most prominent supporters of ragged schools.

(7) 162 ragged day schools closed during the 1870s as the London School Board opened new schools, starting with Old Castle Street, Whitechapel in 1873. Whilst building was in progress, about forty ragged day school premises were used as temporary Board Schools. School attendance was not compulsory to start with and as few fees were remitted many ragged scholars were denied an education when their school was taken over or closed.

Many London children continued to attend National Schools run by the Church of England or British Schools (non-denominational) at about four or six pence a week.

(8) Greater London Record Office: School Admission & Discharge Registers, Dr. Barnardo's Mixed 1886-97.

(9) *Night and Day*, Vol III, 1879 pp 41-42.

(10) *Annual Report* for 1886-87. Barnardo, T. J. *Something Attempted, Something Done!* London 1889, pp 178,233.

(11) *Annual Report* for 1887-88.

(12) *Night and Day*, Vol XIII, 1889 p38.

(13) Free or cheap school meals in London were first provided in Roman Catholic Schools and ragged schools in the early 1860s. The earliest and most

important of the London societies was the Destitute Children's Dinner Society founded in 1864 for feeding ragged school children once or twice a week during the winter. In 1874, Mrs. E. M. Burgwin, Headmistress of Orange Street Board School in Southwark and George Sims of the *Referee* newspaper launched the *Referee* Children's Free Breakfast and Dinner Fund. This was followed by the London Board School Free Dinner Fund in 1882 and the Council for Promoting Self-supporting Penny Dinners in 1884. The London School Board set up the London Schools Dinner Association in 1889 which included most of the voluntary feeding agencies. When the L.C.C. took over London education in 1904 it continued to rely on the voluntary agencies. A scheme for schoolgirls in cookery centres to make cheap meals was started in 1905. The L.C.C. set up Care Committees in 1907 to decide on which children should have a free meal. By 1909 it was providing meals mainly from the rates. A free milk scheme for undernourished children was started in 1910. It was not until the Education Act of 1944 that school meals became an ordinary social service rather than a special service for the needy.

At Hope Place and Copperfield Road, Dr. Barnardo was one of the early pioneers of school meals and was one of the first to provide them on a regular daily basis in the winter months. The *Referee* fund and Dr. Barnardo's Free Meal Branch were the first organisations in London to provide free or cheap breakfasts to poor school children.

(14) From its earliest years the Ragged School Union organised a 'Day in the Country' for its ragged scholars. In 1894, the R.S.U. & Shaftesbury Society (the second title was added the year before) purchased the Retreat at Loughton. This was a large house on the edge of Epping Forest where daily trainloads of up to 1,000 East End schoolchildren were taken in summer. These outings were organised by the R.S.U. & Shaftesbury Society and paid for by Pearson's Fresh Air Fund, originated by C. Arthur Pearson in 1892 in *Pearson's Weekly*.

(15) The Children's Country Holiday Fund was founded by Canon Barnett and his wife Henrietta in 1884. Cyril Jackson was secretary from 1888 to 1896. He was knighted in 1917. The C.C.H.F. is still run from Toynbee Hall.

(16) From 1879, the Deaconesses lived together in one, two then three houses next to one another in Mile End Road. They were Protestant ladies who volunteered to work for Dr. Barnardo, some even paying for their keep. As well as the Factory Girls' Club, they ran Mothers' Meetings at the Edinburgh Castle and Dorcas House in Carr Street and conducted Bible classes in all the various Homes in Stepney. They visited the poor, distributing food and clothing and coal and even lent blankets during cold weather. In 1893 they took up residence at the Edinburgh Castle.

(17) This system of government grant by examination and average attendance was introduced by the Revised Code of 1862. It was known as 'payments by results' and contributed directly to teachers' salaries in elementary schools. The system was revised many times. For example, in 1883 the rule that children had to attend for at least 250 times in the year before examination was changed and all children who had been on the register for six months had to be examined. From 1895 schools could choose to have their grant assessed by one or two unannounced inspections and the system of grant by examination began to disappear. It was not finally abolished in all schools until the code of 1900 which introduced

a single block grant for each school. The old method of examination continued at Copperfield Road until 1901. It has not yet been possible to ascertain what part of the teachers' salaries, if any, depended on the grant.

In contrast, teachers in London's Board Schools ceased to have a direct share in the grant earned by their pupils when the London School Board introduced full fixed salaries in 1883. The Board continued to lead the way in 1890 when grants to schools were based entirely on attendance.

(18) There was also an annual grant of about £50 from the Ragged School Union and the free meals were supplied by Dr. Barnardo's.

(19) The London School Board was an elected body of 49 members representing ten electoral divisions. The Tower Hamlets Division covered the same area as the later Boroughs of Stepney and Poplar. From about 1898 the Divisional Offices were in Harford Street, just the other side of the Regent's Canal from the Copperfield Road Ragged Schools. The building is now used by the Borough of Tower Hamlets. In 1888, Annie Besant was elected to the London School Board as one of the five members for Tower Hamlets. In January 1890, she introduced the successful resolution for free schooling in London. This was followed by the Fee Grant Act of 1891 which made all elementary schools free by a grant of 10s. a year on average attendance for children aged three to fourteen.

(20) British Library of Political and Economic Science: Booth manuscripts.

(21) London Borough of Tower Hamlets: Deeds No. 5132, Architect's Specification August 1895.

(22) *Annual Reports for 1895 and 1896.* St. Ann's Iron Hall was erected in 1875, next to the People's Mission Church in Rhodeswell Road. The Burdett Dormitory was an overflow branch for boys from the Home in Stepney Causeway and the Youths' Labour House in Commercial Road, from 1884 to about 1909. Formerly a mission hall called Burdett Hall which Dr. Barnardo purchased in 1875, it was on the corner of Burdett Road and Dod Street. The site is now part of a block of flats called Leybourne House.

(23) *Annual Report for 1882-83*. The Youths' Labour House or Labour House for Destitute Youths at 626 Commercial Road was established by Dr. Barnardo in 1881 for seventeen to twenty year old vagrants. 622 and 624 Commercial Road were added in 1887. The 200 inmates worked for six months in the saw mill, chopping firewood, making packing cases and bottling lemonade. They were then sent for training to Dr. Barnardo's Industrial Farm in Canada. The Labour House closed in about 1909 when the youths were the first to move to the Boys' Garden City.

(24) *Annual Report for 1882-83.*

(25) Greater London Record Office: School Admission & Discharge Registers, Copperfield Road Boys, 1897-1904. Over a three month period in 1900, about 95 boys from the Boys' Home in Stepney Causeway were admitted and withdrawn from Copperfield Road. The names and addresses of the boys forced to leave in 1904 are crossed out in red ink. The register also contains the names of the boys from Leopold House.

(26) Public Record Office, Kew: Ed 21/12071, 1895-1908, Limehouse Copperfield Road Free School; Ed 30/62, 1884-1909, Stepney: Burdett Road, Leopold House, Dr. Barnardo's Home School.

(27) Dr. Barnardo's planned to reopen Leopold House School which the L.C.C. were prepared to maintain provided alterations were made. Although the Board of Education gave approval, Dr. Barnardo's abandoned their scheme in 1909 and boys from the Home continued to attend local schools until Leopold House was closed in 1911, when the boys were moved to the Boys' Garden City at Woodford Bridge, just three miles from the Girls' Village Home. On Dr. Barnardo's and emigration see Gillian Wagner's *Children of the Empire* (1982).

(28) Public Record Office, Kew: Ed 21/12071, 1895-1908, Limehouse Copperfield Road Free School. The sites of Trafalgar Square and Ocean Street Schools are now occupied by Stepney Green Boys Secondary School. Single Street School was near the junction of Bow Common Lane and Canal Road and the site is now part of Mile End Park. South Grove School to which most of the Leopold House boys went in 1908 had only been built four years earlier and must be one of the last schools to be built by the London School Board. It is now Tower Hamlets Professional Development Centre and is well seen from the upper windows of the Ragged School Museum across Mile End Park and against the background of the trees in Tower Hamlets Cemetery.

(29) *Annual Report for* 1915. This is probably the same W. K. Butler who was master of the Boys' School from 1877. Mr. Douglas was Headmaster in 1905 so presumably Mr. Butler had retired from the Boys' School some time before this, and subsequently took on the superintendence of the Sunday School up to 1915. It was probably Mr. Butler who wrote the report from Copperfield Road in the December 1903 issue of *In His Name*.

(30) For a full list of sponsors and benefactors, see Ragged School Museum Trust Annual Report for 1991-92.

BIBLIOGRAPHY

Annual Reports: *East End Juvenile Mission* (1868-69 to 1875-76)
East End Juvenile Mission, Dr. Barnardo's Homes (1876-77 to 1888)
Dr.Barnardo's Homes (from 1889)
Barnardo, T. J. , *The First Occasional Record of the Lord's Dealings in connexion with the East End Juvenile Mission* (1868)
Barnardo, T. J. , *Something Attempted, Something Done!* (1889)
Broomhall, A. J. , *Hudson Taylor & China's Open Century Book Four: Survivors' Pact* (1984)
Bulkley, M. E. , *The Feeding of School Children* (1914)
Clark, E. A. G., *The Last of the Voluntaryists: The Ragged School Union in the School Board Era* History of Education, 1982, Vol 11, No 1, 23-34
Maclure, S. , *One Hundred Years of London Education 1870-1970* (1970)
Montague, C. J. , *Sixty years in Waifdom or, The Ragged School Movement in English History* (1904)
Night and Day Dr. Barnardo's Homes monthly journal from January 1877
Ridge, T. S. , *Copperfield Road Ragged School*, East London Record (1986)
Royal Commission on Historical Manuscripts, List of Dr. Barnardo's *Child Care Establishments Past and Present* (1979-1982)
Sturt, M. , *The Education of the People* (1967)
Wagner, G. , *Barnardo* (1979)

ACKNOWLEDGEMENTS

Numerous people have helped with my research over the years. In particular, I wish to thank John Nowell and John Potter of Barnardos Library, also Christopher Lloyd and Harry Watton of the Tower Hamlets Local History Library. Sue Elliott of the Shaftesbury Society kindly supplied material from the records of the Ragged School Union. My thanks also to the staff at the Greater London Record Office, Guildhall Library, Department of Education and Science Library, British Library of Political and Economic Science and the Public Record Office at Kew. The drawings from *Night and Day* and the photographs, provided by John Kirkham, are by courtesy of Barnardos. The map of Central Tower Hamlets was adapted from part of the Official Borough Map by Colin Stuart, permission for its use being granted by the Head of Strategic Engineering.

My first history of the Copperfield Road Ragged School appeared in the *East London Record* for 1986. Since then more information has come to light and I am grateful to Colm Kerrigan, the Editor, for permission to reprint parts of that history in this expanded and updated version. My thanks to Pauline Plumb, the Museum's administrator for typing the text; also Isobel Watson for indexing; Jane Straker and Mary Cable for arranging publication; John Finn of Artworkers for design and production assistance.

WHERE TO GO AND WHAT TO SEE

The map on page 34 locates all the places mentioned, except the Free Lodging House in Wapping.

RAGGED SCHOOL MUSEUM

In the last quarter of the nineteenth century, Dr. Barnardo's occupied nearly forty buildings in what is now Tower Hamlets. Of the five still standing, the largest is the Ragged School & Working Lads' Institute in Copperfield Road. This is now the Ragged School Museum. The Museum is about the East End and the history of education and youth provision in London. It is open on Wednesdays and Thursdays (10am to 5pm) and on the first Sunday in the month (2pm to 5pm). Admission is free but donations are appreciated. Schools and groups may book for a Victorian lesson in the recreated classroom (contact the Curator or Administrator on 081-980 6405).

YOUTHS' LABOUR HOUSE

An office block is being built on the site of the three houses on the corner of Commercial Road and Mill Place. However, the three adjacent railway arches and part of the yard where the youths and ragged school boys worked are occupied by a sheet metal works.

SERVANTS' TRAINING HOME

32 Bow Road is a large end-of-terrace house built in the late 1840s and was lived in by Dr. and Mrs. Barnardo from 1875 to 1879, when it was called Newbury House. In 1885 it was re-named Sturge House and became the Servants' Free Registry and Training Home until 1907. It is now divided into flats owned by a housing association.

From 1879 to 1896, the Barnardos lived at The Cedars in Banbury Road, South Hackney. The site is now occupied by a block of flats but one of the brick gateposts is still standing.

CHILDREN'S FOLD

182 Grove Road is a large double fronted villa built about 1880. It is most unusual in that the rear windows have stucco architraves as well as the ones on the front. From 1888 it was Dr. Barnardo's Children's Fold. In its first year it was a hospital for sick cripples but then became a nursery home for boys until 1911. About 1905 it was also referred to as Sheppard House. It is now called Driftway and divided into private flats with an Historic Buildings of Bow plaque on the wall.

FREE LODGING HOUSE

The Free Lodging House at 12 Dock Street, Wapping was in use from 1888 to 1907. It was one of two lodging houses for girls and young women founded by Dr. Barnardo as a safer alternative to the common lodging houses after the 'Whitechapel Murders' of 1888. It is now mainly occupied by shipping companies.

DR. BARNARDO'S LODGINGS

As well as going to see the five surviving Victorian buildings once occupied by Dr. Barnardo's in Tower Hamlets it is worth including two of the surviving Georgian houses Dr. Barnardo lodged in as a young man. His first lodging in London was at 33 Coburn Street but sadly the Historic Buildings of Bow plaque commemorating this has been placed on 30 Coburn Street which was the headquarters of the China Inland Mission. These fine Georgian houses are described as paired villas and were built in the late 1820s on the Morgan Estate. About the same time, the Mercers' Company were starting to build their Estate of mainly two-storey 'cottages' around York Square and Arbour Square, on the north side of Commercial Road. It was at 13 Barnes Street, near York Square, that Barnardo was living when he published his first East End Juvenile Mission report in 1868. The house is now 47 Barnes Street.

HOPE PLACE

The service road between the shops on the south side of Ben Jonson Road was the site of Hope Place. The four houses used by the East End Juvenile Mission were demolished as slums in the late 1930s and the rest of the court was badly blitzed. An L.C.C. blue plaque on Solent House states that it marks the site where Dr. Barnardo began his work for children in 1866. The East End Juvenile Mission was in fact started here in two houses in 1868 but Dr. Barnardo liked to date his work from the cholera epidemic of 1866, preferring to forget that he stayed in Stepney because he was not allowed to go to China. Over thirty years later, Dr. Barnardo described his ragged school as an old donkey shed and it was about this time that a weatherboarded building near the entrance to Hope Place was photographed as the original donkey shed ragged school. The donkey shed story has been repeated by all Barnardo's several biographers, except Gillian Wagner who was the first to examine the contemporary evidence.

STEPNEY CAUSEWAY AND BARNARDO STREET

After Dr. Barnardo's left their offices in Stepney Causeway in 1968, the buildings were demolished to extend the G.L.C. Pitsea Estate. Now the only nineteenth century building is the Royal Duke public house standing at the Commercial Road end of Stepney Causeway. Various Dr. Barnardo establishments lined both sides of this street as far as the railway bridge. The Boys' Home which bore the famous notice NO DESTITUTE CHILD EVER REFUSED ADMISSION, was on the west side and the site is now partly occupied by the block numbered 1-20 Lipton Road. On the east side, the main building was Her Majesty's Hospital for Sick Children, the site of which is now occupied by Ogilvie House. This has a bronze plaque fixed by the G.L.C. in 1983 which states "Dr. Barnardo's first home for boys stood on this site 1870-1970". It should have been fixed on the 1-20 Lipton Road block on the opposite side of the Causeway.

The Boys' Home playground was at the back and at the side of the Home next to the railway viaduct and extended under two of the arches. One of these was the nearest arch to the west of the

Stepney Causeway bridge and is still in use as a children's playground. Under the arch, it is noticeable that there is an old broad arch in the middle with newer narrower arches on either side. The middle part was the original London & Blackwall Railway viaduct built in 1839 - the East End's second oldest railway viaduct and subsequently widened to three then four tracks.

The site of the Boys' Home School in Bower Street, and Bower Street itself, is now partly occupied by blocks numbered 1-20 and 39-52 Lipton Road. The new Bower Street still runs north-south but is further west and curves back eastwards to go under the old Bower Street railway arch which leads through to Barnardo Street. This was formerly Ann Street and renamed in Dr. Barnardo's honour in 1911.

EDINBURGH CASTLE

The Mile End Stadium Car Park in Rhodeswell Road was the site of the Edinburgh Castle, the People's Mission Church and St. Ann's Iron Hall. At the Castle, Dr. Barnardo kept the original saloon bar for the sale of coffee, cocoa and tea. The Church was completely rebuilt in 1883 and the Castle became the centre for most of the relief agencies. Dr. Barnardo's left in 1927 and the premises were leased to the East End Mission. They were demolished in the clearance for new playing fields, opened in 1952 as King George's Fields. The East London Stadium was built in the Fields and its name subsequently changed to Mile End Stadium.

WOODCHOPPING BRIGADE

The children's playground to the north of Jacobs House, off Carr Street, partly occupies the site of Rhodeswell Wharf which was used by the Woodchopping Brigade from 1873 to 1883.

LEOPOLD HOUSE

The tower block on the Leopold Estate on the corner of Burdett Road and Ackroyd Avenue occupies the site of Leopold House. It is named Elmslie Point. Elmslie was Mrs. Barnardo's maiden name. Her brother, Harry Elmslie, was the Chief Steward of Dr. Barnardo's Homes.

Central Tower Hamlets:
Dr. Barnardo's main institutions and two houses in which he lodged
ADAPTED FROM THE OFFICIAL BOROUGH MAP

Buildings
1. Ragged School & Working Lads' Institute
2. Youths' Labour House
3. Servants' Training Home
4. Children's Fold
5. 33 Coburn Street
6. 47 Barnes Street

Sites
7. Hope Place
8. Boys' Home, Stepney Causeway
9. Edinburgh Castle
10. Woodchopping Brigade
11. Leopold House

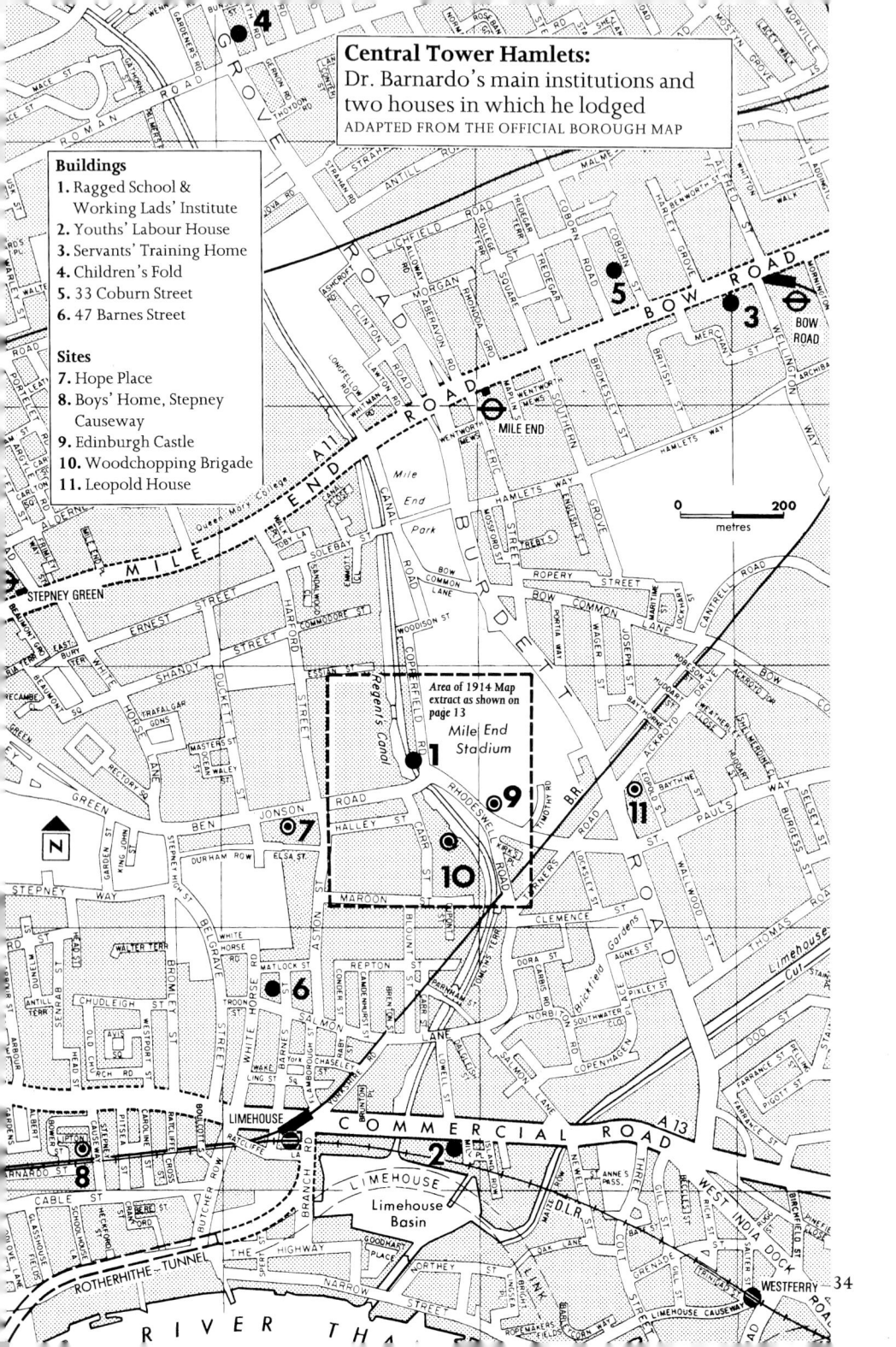

Area of 1914 Map extract as shown on page 13

INDEX

Ackroyd Avenue 33
Ann Street 33

Banbury Road 30
Bands of Hope, Copperfield Road 18
Barnardo Street 33
Barnardo, Syrie 3, 20, 30, 33
Barnardo, Thomas John *passim*, and:
    early life 2
    lodgings in East End 31, 34
    founds East End Juvenile Mission 2
    marriage 3
    residences in East End 30
    dispute as to title Doctor 3
    founds Copperfield Road Ragged Schools 3-4
    death and funeral 19
Barnes Street 31, 34
Barnett, Samuel and Henrietta 25
Ben Jonson Road 32
Besant, Annie 26
bible classes 9, 25
Bilbie, Mr. J. 9
Board of Education 19, 27
Board Schools 5, 6, 11, 12, 18, 24, 25
Booth, Charles 12
Bow Road 17, 30
Bower Street 33
Boys' Homes
    Boys' Garden City, Woodford Bridge 26-27
    Children's Fold, Grove Road 31, 34
    Leopold House, Burdett Road 19-20, 26-27, 33, 34
    Stepney Causeway (founded as Home for Working and Destitute Lads) 2, 3, 16, 17, 26, 32-33, 34
British Schools (non-denominational) 24
Brown, Elizabeth 24
Bryant and May's factory 16
Burdett Dormitory 14, 26
Burdett Road 4, 7-8, 19, 26, 33
Burdett-Coutts, Baroness 4, 24
Burgwin, Mrs. E. M. 25
Burrell, Jane 12
Butler, Sarah 4, 6, 24
Butler, W. K. 4, 6, 21, 24, 27

Cairns, Lord 3
Canada, emigration to 19-20, 26, 27
Carr Street 13, 15, 18, 25, 33
casual work 6, 17

Cedars, Banbury Road 30
Charity Organisation Society 12
Charrington, Frederick 3
Children's Country Holiday Fund 9, 25
China Inland Mission, Bow headquarters 2, 31
cholera outbreak, 1866 2, 32
City Messenger Brigade 15, 16
clothing manufacturers, Copperfield Road 22
clothing, provision of 6, 14
Coburn Street 31, 34
Copperfield Road
    fire in 22
    Mission School, *see* Edinburgh Castle Mission School
    name, origin of 4
    Ragged Schools, *see* ragged schools, Copperfield Road
    renumbering 22
    warehouses 4, 12, 22
    Working Lads' Institute 9-10, 12, 13, 14, 22, 23, 30, 34
Council for Promoting Self-supporting Penny Dinners 25
Crosse, Henry 12

Deaconess House, Mile End Road 9
Deaconesses, Dr. Barnardo's 8, 13, 17, 25
Destitute Children's Dinner Society 6, 25
Dick, W. R. & Sons Ltd. 22
Dickens, Charles 4, 24
Dock Street 31
Dod Street 26
domestic service, training for 17
"Donkey Row" (Carr Street) 13, 18
Dorcas House, Carr Street 13, 25
Douglas, Mr. 27
Driftway, Grove Road 31

Earee, John, of Hackney Road 9
'East End', first use of term 24
East End Juvenile Mission 2, 3, 31-32
East End Mission 33
East End Relief Association 6
Edinburgh Castle, Limehouse 3, 4, 13, 18, 19, 21, 25, 33, 34
Edinburgh Castle Mission School 20-21
Education Acts 5, 6, 18, 19, 26
Ellman, J., & Son Ltd. 22
Elmslie, Syrie *see* Barnardo, Syrie
Elmslie, Harry 33

Elmslie Point 33
emigration to Canada 19-20, 26, 27
Epping Forest 7, 25
Ernest Street, Mile End 2
exercise 10, 18, 19

Factory Girls' Club & Institute 8, 9, 17, 18, 21, 25
factory workers 9, 16-17, 20
fees for schooling 5, 11, 24, 26
Free Lodging House, Dock Street 30, 31
Fresh Air Fund, Dr. Barnardo's 9, 25
    see also Pearson's Fresh Air Fund

Girls' Village Home, Barkingside 3, 19-20, 27
Gregg, Ebenezer 12
Grove Road 31

Harford Street, Mile End 2, 26
Harris & Woolf 22
Her Majesty's Hospital for Sick Children 32
Her Majesty's Inspectors 10, 12
Hewett, George 4
homeless children, Spitalfields 2
Hope Place 2, 3, 6, 15, 25, 32, 34
housing conditions, Limehouse Fields 11

inspection of schools 10, 12, 25-26
Institutional Schools 19

Jackson, Cyril 25
Jarvis, Jim 2

Kennedy, Miss 17
King George's Fields 33

Leybourne House 26
Limehouse Fields 4, 11, 13, 18
Lipton Road 32-33
Local Government Board 19
lodging houses for girls, Dr. Barnardo's 30, 31
London & Blackwall Railway 33
London Board School Free Dinner Fund 25
London City Mission 24
London County Council 18, 20, 25, 27
    schools 20, 27
London Education Act 1903 18
London Hospital, Barnardo's studies at 2
London School Board 5, 24, 25, 26, 27
    see also Board Schools
London Schools Dinner Association 25
Loughton, R.S.U. Retreat at 25

Macpherson, Annie 2
match factories, workers in 9, 16

Mayhew, Henry 24
Mercers' Company Estate 31
Mile End Park, proposed extension to 22
Mile End Stadium 33
milk, provision of in schools 25
model dwellings 11
Mothers' Meetings 13, 25

National Schools (Church of England) 24
Newbury House 30
Newman, Ann 4, 24
Night and Day 7, 21, 24, 28

Ocean Street, temporary school at 20, 27
occupations, Limehouse Fields 11
Ogilvie House 32

payment for schooling 5, 11, 26
Pearson, C. Arthur 25
Pearson's Fresh Air Fund 9, 25
People's Mission Church (from 1873, also referred to as
    the Edinburgh Castle) 3, 4, 13, 26, 33
Pitsea Estate 32
Privy Council on Education 10

Ragged School Museum and Trust 21, 23, 30
Ragged School Union 4, 17, 24, 25
ragged schools 2, 24
    Copperfield Road 3-14, 17-21, 26, 30
        admission registers 5
        alteration and extension 12, 14
        attendance 4, 11-12, 14, 25
        bell 14, 22
        Board of Education, dispute with 19
        Boys' School 4, 14
        cleanliness of children 12
        closure by L.C.C 18, 20
        discipline 10, 12
        employment of ex-pupils 14-18
        emigration of pupils 19-20
        evening classes 9-10, 14, 18, 20
        Girls' and Infants' School 12, 13, 14, 23
        grants for 10, 25
        holidays, provision of 9, 14, 25
        hop-picking season, effect of 12, 15
        illustrations/maps *front cover*, 5, 6, 7, 8, 13,
            21, 34
        inspection of 10, 12, 25-26
        meals, provision of 6-7, 11, 14, 25
        numbers on register 4, 11, 14, 18, 20
        outings to Theydon Bois 7-9
        recognition by Government 10
        report from, in 1903 17
        standards 10

ragged schools *continued*
    subjects taught 10
    Sunday schools 4, 7, 9, 14, 18, 20-21
    teachers 4, 10, 14, 18, 24
    voluntary contributions for 10
  Ernest Street 2
  Field Lane 24
  George Yard, Whitechapel 20
  Hope Place 2, 3, 6, 15, 25, 32, 34
  Salmon Lane 3
Referee Children's Free Breakfast and Dinner Fund 6, 25
Regent's Canal 4, 13, 15, 26
Reynolds, George 3
Rhodeswell Road 3, 8, 13, 26, 33
Rhodeswell Wharf, Carr Street 15, 33
Roman Catholic Schools, provision of meals by 24
Royal College of Surgeons, Edinburgh 3
Royal Duke public house 32

St. Ann's Iron Hall 13, 14, 26, 33
St. Thomas's Road 8
schooling, payment for 5, 11, 24, 26
Selfridge, H. Gordon 21
Servants' Free Registry and Training Home 17, 30, 34
Shaftesbury, Lord 3, 4, 24
Sheppard House 31
Shoreditch, model dwellings in 11
Sims, George 25
Single Street School 20, 27
Solent House 32
Somerset, Duke and Duchess of 20
South Grove School 20, 27
Spitalfields, homeless children in 2
Stepney, cholera in 2, 32
Stepney Causeway 2, 3, 16, 17, 26, 32-33, 34
Stepney Green School 27
"street arabs" 2
Sturge House 30

Taylor, Dr. Hudson 2
Trafalgar Square School, Stepney 20, 27

unemployment 6, 17

Victory Bridge 8, 13
Village Home for Girls, Barkingside 3, 19-20, 27

Wagner, Lady 23, 32
Westall, Robert 4
White Estate 4
Whitechapel, model dwellings in 11
Winn, J. H. 21
Woodchopping Brigade 13, 15, 33, 34
Working Men's Club and Coffee Palace 3, 33

Working Lads' Institute, Copperfield Road 9-10, 12, 13, 14, 22, 23, 30, 34
World's End, Limehouse 2
Youths' Labour House, Commercial Road 15-16, 26, 30, 34

37

RAGGED SCHOOL MUSEUM

The museum in the East End about the East End and the history of Education and Youth Provision in London in buildings which once housed the largest Ragged School in London.

Open on Wednesdays and Thursdays 10.00am - 5.00pm
First Sunday in the month 2.00pm - 5.00pm
ADMISSION FREE • DONATIONS APPRECIATED

The museum collects the ordinary things of daily life, school, work and leisure and is always pleased to hear from people with items to donate or lend.

The museum is registered by the Museums and Galleries Commission. It is owned and run by the Ragged School Museum Trust, which is a registered charity and company limited by guarantee, funded by the London Boroughs Grants Committee, London Docklands Development Corporation, London Borough of Tower Hamlets, London East Training and Enterprise Council and other benefactors.

Membership of the Trust is open to all and there is a wide range of activities, including a history club which meets on the second Wednesday evening during the winter months. The Trust is most anxious to hear from people interested in helping as guides or in the shop or cafe. If you would like to become a member or help in any way, please send a stamped, addressed envelope to RSMT Secretary, 46-50 Copperfield Road, Bow, London E3 4RR or telephone the Curator or Administrator on 020 8980 6405.

Patrons of the Ragged School Museum Trust
Dame Gillian Wagner DBE
Lord Briggs
Bruce Oldfield
Lord Murray